PETER KENT

HIDDEN UNDER THE GROUND

THE WORLD BENEATH YOUR FEET

DUTTON CHILDREN'S BOOKS ◆ NEW YORK

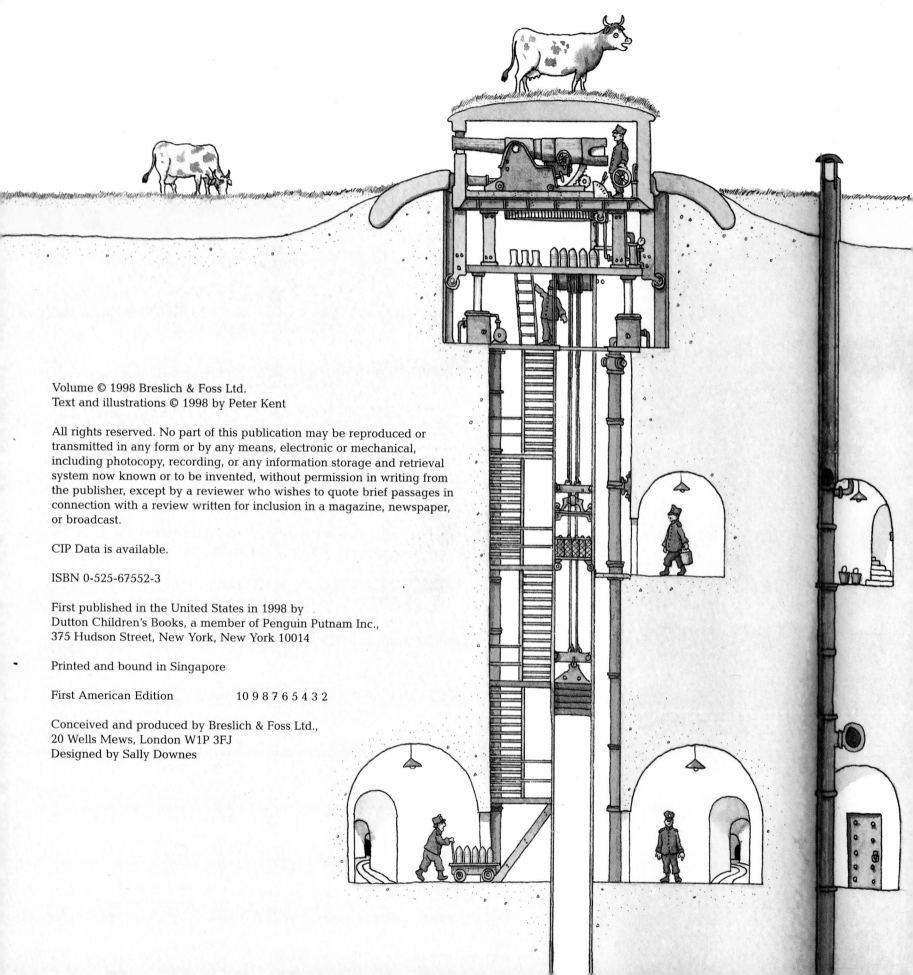

Volume © 1998 Breslich & Foss Ltd.
Text and illustrations © 1998 by Peter Kent

CIP Data is available.

ISBN 0-525-67552-3

First published in the United States in 1998 by
Dutton Children's Books, a member of Penguin Putnam Inc.,
375 Hudson Street, New York, New York 10014

Printed and bound in Singapore

First American Edition   10 9 8 7 6 5 4 3 2

Conceived and produced by Breslich & Foss Ltd.,
20 Wells Mews, London W1P 3FJ
Designed by Sally Downes

CONTENTS

GOING UNDERGROUND

There are many reasons for going underground. In prehistoric times, some people lived in caves, but the first reason that people dug and tunneled underground was to reach valuable minerals that could not be found on the surface. Four thousand years ago, miners in England dug down to reach the best flints. The ancient Egyptians tunneled into the rocks for gold. Since then, millions of miles of mine tunnels have been dug, and billions of tons of useful minerals have been brought to the surface.

Another reason for going underground is security. Treasure and prisoners have often been held safe in deep vaults. Underground is a good place to escape extremes of weather and the dangers of war. As guns became more powerful, soldiers copied moles and built forts underground. Once aircraft carried bombs, no one was safe above ground. During World War II, people took refuge from bombs in large public air-raid shelters or in small shelters in their yards. Governments built huge bunkers to protect their headquarters. Both Winston Churchill, the prime minister of Britain during World War II, and Adolf Hitler, the leader of Germany, had underground command centers. After the invention of nuclear weapons, governments dug even deeper and planned shelters in which a few people could survive underground after every living thing above ground had been destroyed.

Secrecy is another part of security, and there are many secret places underground, most of them designed for military purposes. Many secret societies have used caves to meet in. The first Christians in Rome held their services in the catacombs.

Lack of space is a good reason for going underground. In cities, buildings are so tightly packed that extra space can be gained only by digging down. All the services that keep the city going—pipes and cables for gas, electricity, water, and telecommunications—run below the streets. Every day millions of people travel in speed and comfort in trains under streets that are full of cars. Many cars are parked underground. More cities are building underground shopping malls, and in some places it is now possible to spend a whole day shopping, working, and traveling without coming to the surface.

SUBTERRANEAN CELEBRITIES

Hades was the god of the underworld in Greek mythology. He lived in an underground palace with his wife, Persephone, whom he had kidnapped from above ground. All the precious metals and gems in the earth were said to belong to him.

The Minotaur was a monster, half man and half bull, that lived in the labyrinth beneath the palace at Knossos on Crete. He was killed by Theseus, who found his way out of the monster's lair by following a thread that led back to the entrance.

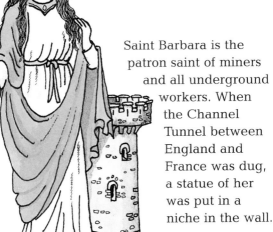

Saint Barbara is the patron saint of miners and all underground workers. When the Channel Tunnel between England and France was dug, a statue of her was put in a niche in the wall.

There are many legends of ancient heroes who sleep beneath the ground, waiting to emerge and save their country when it is in great danger. King Wenceslaus of Bohemia (about 903–935), the "Good King" of the Christmas carol, is supposed to sleep beneath a rock near Prague, and the mythical King Arthur is said to rest under Glastonbury Tor, a hill in the west of England.

A girl was born in a train on the Bakerloo Underground, or "Tube," line in London. She was christened Thelma Ursula Beatrice Eleanor, so that her initials would be a reminder of her birthplace.

Bernard Isaac lived for 11 years below the streets of New York in a subway tunnel. During the 1970s there were more than 5,000 people living underground in the city.

The eccentric 5th duke of Portland built underground extensions to his country mansion at Welbeck, in England. They included stables, a subterranean ballroom, and miles (kilometers) of underground roads, so he could drive to the railroad station without being seen.

Professor William Boyd-Dawkins was one of the pioneers of cave exploration, or spelunking, in England. He encouraged others to explore and map the limestone caves of North Yorkshire and wrote the first book on the subject of potholes, *Cave Hunting*, which was published in 1874.

Germain Sommeiller was the engineer of the great Mount Cenis railroad tunnel beneath the Alps, between Switzerland and France. He developed many new techniques of tunneling and finished the work in 14 years, well ahead of the estimated 25!

AFTERLIFE UNDERWORLDS

In ancient times, people had very little knowledge of what lay underground. From cave explorations, they knew the place was dark and cold, but people who lived near volcanoes suspected it might be full of fire. Legends grew about a separate underworld inhabited by strange monsters where people went after they died. The Greeks believed in a gloomy kingdom of the underworld ruled by the god Hades. Other ancient peoples had similar beliefs.

Medieval artists imagined devils to be foul, dark and ugly – the opposite of angels, who were supposed to be beautiful and bright.

Lazy people were forced to engage in never-ending activity.

The worst torments were reserved for extremely wicked people.

Satan was the ruler of Hell.

In the center of hell, there was supposed to be a lake of burning fire that never went out.

In the Middle Ages, all Christians believed that hell lay beneath the earth. Hell was the home of Satan and a horde of devils, where the souls of wicked people went after death to be punished for eternity. Artists in the Middle Ages often painted pictures of hell similar to this one.

How many kings, queens and knights can you see?

People who drank too much on earth were punished by eternal thirst.

Creatures of the Underworld

The Greeks and Romans believed that the underworld was guarded by a terrible three-headed dog called Cerberus. It stopped the living from entering and the dead from leaving.

The Egyptian god of the underworld—always shown with a jackal's head—was Anubis.

In Greek mythology, the singer Orpheus followed his wife, Eurydice—after her death—down to the underworld. With his music he got past Cerberus and charmed Hades into letting her go. The one condition Hades made was that Orpheus must not look back to see if Eurydice was following him. Just as they were about to leave the underworld, Orpheus looked around, and Eurydice was lost forever.

CAVES AND CAVERNS

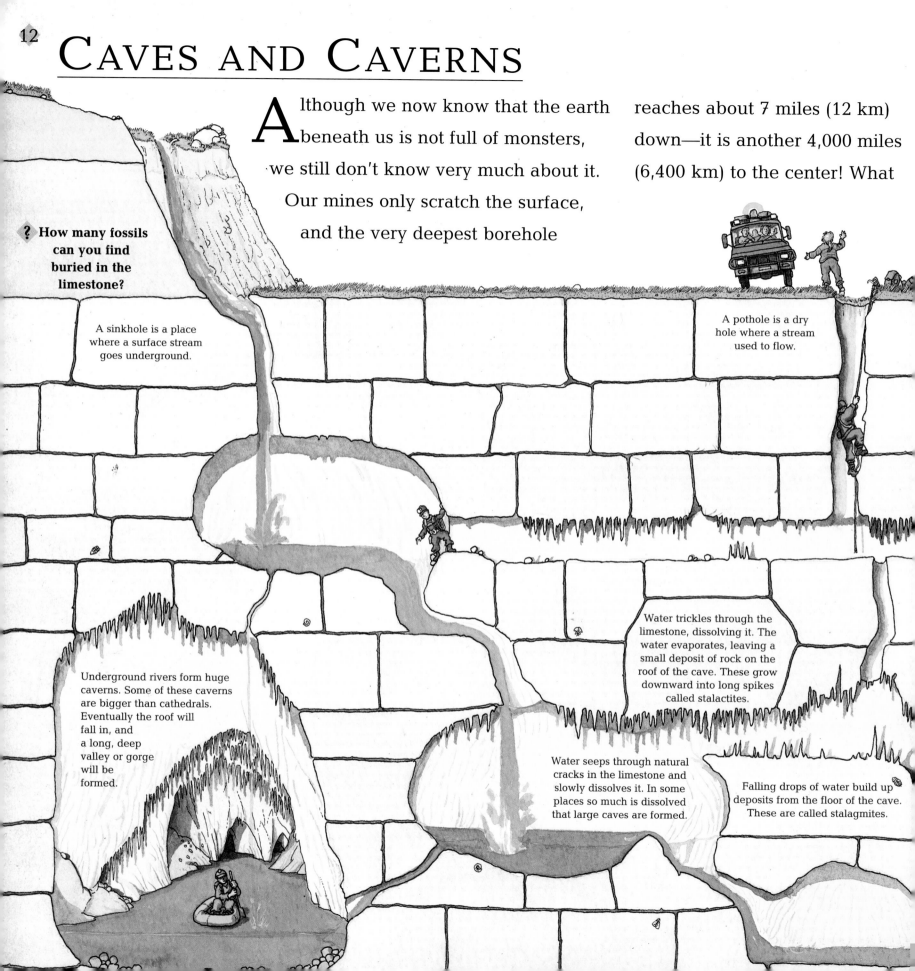

Although we now know that the earth beneath us is not full of monsters, we still don't know very much about it. Our mines only scratch the surface, and the very deepest borehole reaches about 7 miles (12 km) down—it is another 4,000 miles (6,400 km) to the center! What

? How many fossils can you find buried in the limestone?

A sinkhole is a place where a surface stream goes underground.

A pothole is a dry hole where a stream used to flow.

Underground rivers form huge caverns. Some of these caverns are bigger than cathedrals. Eventually the roof will fall in, and a long, deep valley or gorge will be formed.

Water trickles through the limestone, dissolving it. The water evaporates, leaving a small deposit of rock on the roof of the cave. These grow downward into long spikes called stalactites.

Water seeps through natural cracks in the limestone and slowly dissolves it. In some places so much is dissolved that large caves are formed.

Falling drops of water build up deposits from the floor of the cave. These are called stalagmites.

we do know is that most of the earth is white-hot molten rock and metal under immense pressure and that the core is probably made largely of iron and nickel. Scientists who study the earth and its rocks are known as geologists.

This picture shows what it is like underground in a region made up of limestone rocks.

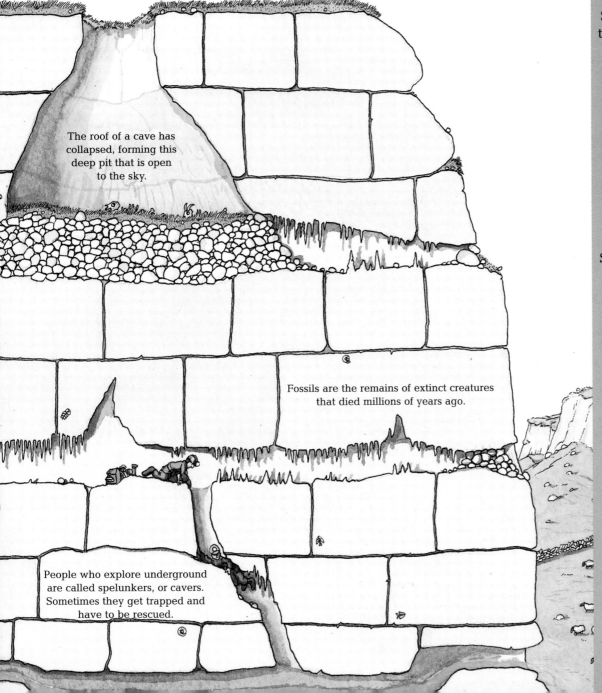

The roof of a cave has collapsed, forming this deep pit that is open to the sky.

Fossils are the remains of extinct creatures that died millions of years ago.

People who explore underground are called spelunkers, or cavers. Sometimes they get trapped and have to be rescued.

Cave Curiosities

Some caves were lived in by people in prehistoric times. They left paintings of hunting scenes on the walls. These are the first pictures made by humankind, and some are 17,000 years old.

Strange white—almost transparent—fish and frogs live in underground rivers where no light ever penetrates. They are blind because there is no light, so they don't need eyes.

One of the largest caves in the world is Mammoth Cave in Kentucky. It is 4 miles (6.5 km) long and 40 ft. (12 m) high.

ANIMAL UNDERWORLD

Many animals and insects live underground for reasons of comfort and safety. A burrow in the earth keeps them dry and warm, or cool, and once they are inside, their enemies cannot reach them. Most of these animals go underground only to sleep or to escape predators, but some spend all their lives beneath the surface. There are all sorts of underground animal homes, from simple holes scraped into a bank to complex tunnel systems that extend for hundreds of yards (meters).

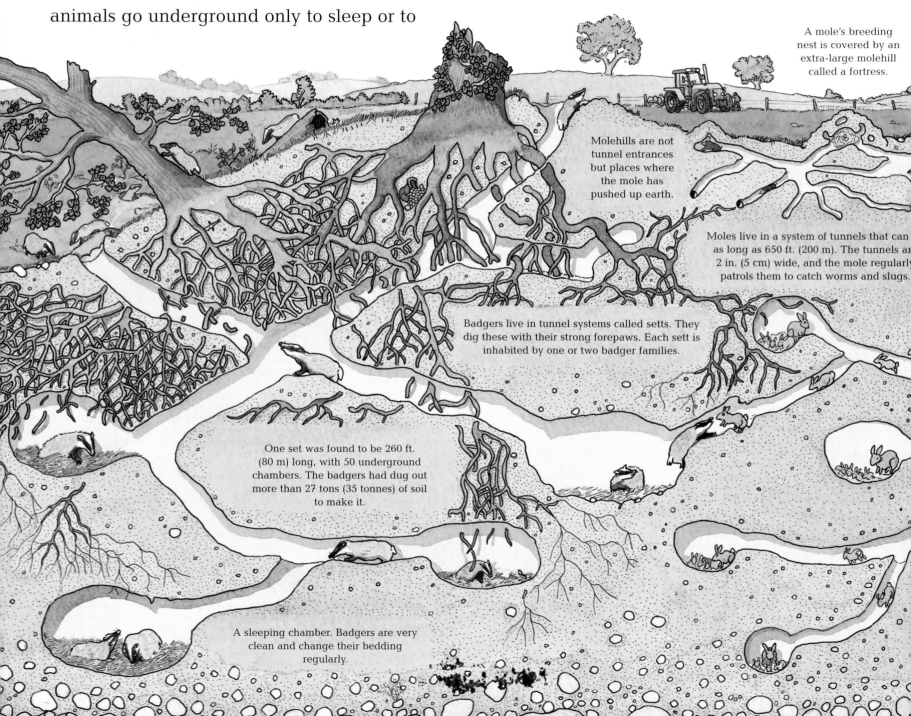

A mole's breeding nest is covered by an extra-large molehill called a fortress.

Molehills are not tunnel entrances but places where the mole has pushed up earth.

Moles live in a system of tunnels that can as long as 650 ft. (200 m). The tunnels ar 2 in. (5 cm) wide, and the mole regularl patrols them to catch worms and slugs.

Badgers live in tunnel systems called setts. They dig these with their strong forepaws. Each sett is inhabited by one or two badger families.

One set was found to be 260 ft. (80 m) long, with 50 underground chambers. The badgers had dug out more than 27 tons (35 tonnes) of soil to make it.

A sleeping chamber. Badgers are very clean and change their bedding regularly.

624.1   Kent, Peter.
KEN   Hidden under the
          ground

PERMA-BOUND   BAR: 3271078064867

DATE DUE			

$21.14